THE DAY THE WOMEN GOT THE VOTE

A Photo History of the Women's Rights Movement

by George Sullivan

SCHOLASTIC INC.
New York Toronto London Auckland Sydney

Cover Photos

Front cover: (top right) March in support of the ERA, Washington, DC, 1977—Washington *Star* Collection, Martin Luther King Library; (clockwise from middle left) World War II WACs—National Archives; A woman working in an area formerly closed to women—AP/Wide World; Jackie Joyner Kersee displays the second gold medal she won in the 1988 Olympic Games—AP/Wide World; Eleanor Roosevelt, May 14, 1958—UPI/Bettman; Susan B. Anthony—AP/Wide World.

Back cover: Suffragists in 1912—UPI/Bettmann.

Interior Photo Credits

Pages 4, 5 (top), 11, 52, 65, 73, and 79 (inset)—UPI/Bettman. Pages 5 (bottom), 7, 8 (right), 9, 15 (right), 17 (left), 19, 21, 23, 24 (bottom), 28, 31, 35, 36, 38, 40 (left), 41 (left), 50 (left), 51, 53, and 54 (right)—Library of Congress. Pages 6, 55, 57, 62, 63, 64 (right), 66, 68, 69, 70, 71, 72, 75, 76, 77, 78, 79, 80, 81, 82 (top), 84, 85, 86, and 88—AP/Wide World. Pages 8 (left), 12, 13 (inset), 15 (left), 18, and 41 (right)—New York Public Library. Pages 10, 25 (right), 29 (left), 40 (right), and 67 (bottom)—George Sullivan. Page 14—Mount Holyoke College. Page 13—Emma Willard School. Pages 16, 43 (inset), 44, 45, 59, and 60—National Archives. Page 17 (right)—Fall River Historical Society. Pages 20, 24 (top), 32, and 37—Sophia Smith Collection; Smith College. Pages 22 and 27—Seneca Falls Historical Society. Pages 25 (left), 26, 29 (right), and 33—Alberti/Lowe Collection. Page 30—San Francisco Public Library. Pages 34, 64 (left), and 67 (top)—Washington *Star* Collection; Martin Luther King Library. Page 42—Lewis Hine/National Archives. Page 43—International Museum of Photography. Page 46—Spelman College. Pages 47 and 49—Gordon Parks/Library of Congress. Page 48—Bethune-Cookman College. Page 50 (right)—London Museum. Page 54 (left)—Sy Kessler. Pages 56 and 58—Franklin D. Roosevelt Library. Page 61—Queensboro Public Library; New York *Herald Tribune* Collection. Page 82 (bottom)—Office of Barbara Mikulski. Page 83—Office of Carol Mosely Braun.

Acknowledgments

A great many people helped the author by suggesting sources of information for this book, vetting portions of the manuscript, and providing photographs, reproductions of engravings, and other art. Special thanks are due the following: Susan Griffith and Amelia Fry, National Woman's Party; Carla Williams, Schomberg Center for Research in Black Culture; William Leonard and Fran Barberry, Seneca Falls Historical Society; Mary Ternes, Washington Star Collection, Martin Luther King Memorial Library; Araina Heath, Sophia Smith Collection, Smith College; Catherine A. Kershaw, Bethune-Cookman College; Robin MacKenzie Johnson, Emma Willard School; Manet Davis, National Coalition of 100 Black Women; G. E. Morgan, Museum of London; Deborah Collins and Dennis A. Binette, Fall River Historical Association; Sandra Hoeh-Lyon, University of Wisconsin — Milwaukee; Daile Kaplan, Swann Galleries; Mandy Szkotak, Mount Holyoke College; Charles Young and William Asadorian, Long Island Division, Queensboro Public Library; Andrea Ashmore, Spelman College; Patricia Sarles, Brooklyn Public Library; Francesca Kurti, TLC Labs; James Lowe and Sal Alberti; Tim and Frances Sullivan, and Sy Kessler.

Book and Cover Design by Dawn Antoniello

ISBN 0-590-47560-6

Copyright © 1994 by George Sullivan.
All rights reserved. Published by Scholastic Inc.

12 11 10 9 8 7 6 5 4 3 2 1   4 5 6 7 8 9/9

Printed in the U.S.A.   34

First Scholastic printing, March 1994

TABLE OF CONTENTS

Women protested and marched for years before being granted equal voting rights. Here a flag-bearing marcher is pictured about 1910.

4

Members of the Women's Congressional Union for Equal Suffrage storm the Capitol in 1916.

A delegation of women speak out for suffrage before the Judiciary Committee of Congress in 1871.

Great Day

Tuesday, November 2, 1920. To *The New York Times*, it was "the greatest voting day in the City's history."

It was not just in New York. In every city and state, it was a day of triumph. For the first time in history, American women, most of whom had never before been permitted to vote in a presidential election, headed for the polling places. In voting booths, at least, women had achieved equality with men.

Women in most states of the United States had been denied the right to vote for well over a century. Many of those who were opposed to women voting believed that a woman's place was in the home. Her role was to marry, keep house, have children, raise them, and have nothing to do with her husband's business or profession. It was said that

5

Women marchers appealed to President Woodrow Wilson with banner reading: HOW LONG MUST WOMEN WAIT FOR LIBERTY.

once women started to become involved in politics it would lead to an end of family life.

Women waged a long and often bitter struggle to win voting rights. They marched and picketed and went on hunger strikes. Often they were arrested and jailed.

Thanks to their efforts, an amendment to the Constitution was introduced in Congress in 1878. It says: "The right of citizens of the United States to vote shall not be denied or abridged by the United States or by any State, on account of sex."

The amendment was defeated.

It was reintroduced in every session of Congress for the next 40 years. Not until 1918 did the House of Representatives approve it. The Senate passed the amendment in 1919 and sent it to the states for approval. A Constitutional amendment has to be ratified by three fourths of the states to become law.

A suffrage parade in New York in 1915.

In 1920, when women finally won voting rights equal to those of men, this newspaper drawing hailed "The end of the climb."

For picketing the White House on behalf of women's suffrage, the militant Alice Paul was arrested and imprisoned.

On August 18, 1920, Tennessee became the thirty-sixth state to ratify the amendment. It was declared to be the law, the Nineteenth Amendment to the Constitution, on August 26, 1920. The long fight was over.

In the presidential campaign of 1920, Senator Warren G. Harding, the Republican candidate, who was heavily favored to win, remained at his Marion, Ohio, home, greeting patriotic groups, party bosses, and campaign workers on the front porch. Newspaper reporters assigned to cover Harding hung around, chatting with him. "Harding is a regular fellow," said one. "He doesn't use fancy language and he's no intellectual. He's just plain folks . . . "

While Harding rocked on the porch, James M. Cox, the Democratic nominee, campaigned hard. He traveled some 22,000 miles (quite a feat, considering commercial air travel was several years away) and spoke to two million people in an effort to draw support.

As expected, Harding scored a lopsided victory. The Ohio senator won 60 percent of the popular vote — 16,152,200 to Cox's 9,147,353. "It wasn't a landslide," said a Harding staff member. "It was an earthquake."

In the electoral count, Harding got

8

404 votes to Cox's 127. Women voted just as overwhelmingly for men as Harding.

The fact that women had the right to vote made only a slight change in their actual status. For instance, while they could vote, they had only men to vote for. In local, state, and national elections, women political candidates were a great rarity.

Women faced many barriers. They were denied jobs and unable to enter a number of professions.

A woman could become a school teacher, librarian, or nurse. She might find work as a salesclerk in a department store, a bookkeeper in a bank, or as a typist or stenographer. Women also worked in mills and did light factory work. But most professions were closed to women. Only on rare occasions did a woman become a doctor or a lawyer, an architect or engineer. And many colleges and universities rejected women solely because they were women.

Winning the vote was important to women. But it was only one step on the long road they traveled in an effort to achieve social, economic, legal, and political rights equal to those of men.

Determined suffragists stand at the gates of the White House.

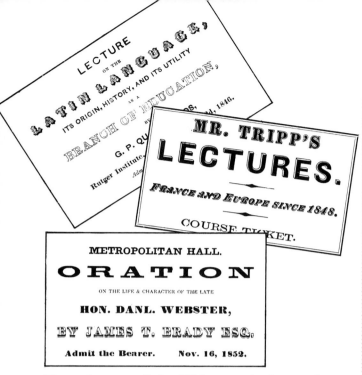

Through most of the 1800s, people frequently attended lectures for information and entertainment. Men did the lecturing, not women.

Speaking Out

Long before American women began their long fight for equal voting rights, there were female rebels in the United States. Since women traditionally had fewer rights and a lower social status than men, and were believed by many to be less intelligent than men, there was plenty to be rebellious about.

State and federal law reflected the idea of women's inferiority. Women were not only banned from voting but were not permitted to sit on juries or own property. If a woman was married, her husband had control of her earnings.

Mary Wollstonecraft, a British writer, was one of the first women to speak out for equal rights and opportunities. She wanted to change the relationship between men and women. Instead of women being dependent on men, she wanted equality. In her essay, *A Vindication of the Rights of Women*, published in 1792, she said, "I do not wish [women] to have power over men, but over themselves." She also called for greater educational opportunities for women.

Mary Wollstonecraft's essay was widely read by American women who felt there was something wrong with the way they were treated by society. Many of these women were active in the anti-slavery movement. These women, however, had no power even as abolitionists.

In the days before television, radio, and other forms of electronic mass communication, people often attended lectures for information and entertainment. Men did the lecturing, however, not women. Women who were active as abolitionists were expected to preach their anti-slavery message only to other women. They could not vote at organizational meetings of abolitionist societies. They had no leadership role. These women soon came to realize that they themselves were victims.

Two sisters from Charleston, South Carolina, daughters of one of the South's most respected families, helped to bring what came to be called "the woman question" into sharper focus. Sarah and Angelina Grimké were brought up on a large plantation and were in close touch with slavery every day of their lives. The sight of "bad" slaves being beaten sickened them. Slavery, they realized, was at odds with the Quaker concepts of morality they were being taught.

The Grimké sisters became active in the abolitionist movement. In 1836 and 1837, they toured much of the Northeast, often speaking to huge audiences about slavery's horrors. Many people criticized them for speaking out on public issues. It was considered "unnatural" behavior for women. Even Catherine Beecher, a noted educational reformer of the time, joined in the criticism, rebuking the sisters for abandoning the "women's sphere"— the home.

The sisters were quick to defend their right to organize and speak. They pointed out the close connection between enslaved blacks and white women. "If we do not have the right to act," they said, "then may we well be termed 'the white slaves of the North.' "

Early in 1838, Angelina Grimké addressed the legislature of the state of

Sarah Grimké (above), along with her sister Angelina, were among the first women to speak out for women's rights.

Through early 1800s, women were expected to learn domestic tasks—and little else.

Massachusetts. She presented the legislators with anti-slavery petitions signed by 20,000 women. Her address marked the first time a woman had ever spoken before a legislative body in the United States. It was a turning point in women's long experience of public silence.

The movement to abolish slavery wasn't the only cause to attract women activists of the time. They also sought property rights for women, greater educational opportunities for young girls, and voting rights for women, called suffrage.

The belief that women should have social, economic, legal, and political equality with men is often called feminism. According to Alice Rossi, a modern-day sociologist, and also a writer and editor, the term feminism was first used in a book review published in *The Athenaeum* on April 27, 1895. Women who worked for women's rights came to be known as feminists. Both terms were in widespread use by the early 1900s.

Modern campus buildings at the Emma Willard School in Troy, New York.

In Troy, New York, in 1821, Emma Willard founded the first institution of higher learning for girls.

Women and Education

During the early decades of the 1800s, as pioneers pushed the nation's borders west, the concept of free education went with them and eventually stretched from one coast to the other. It was believed that every voter needed to be responsible and informed. The right to an education was regarded as basic as free speech.

But education for girls beyond elementary school was available only to the well-to-do. What was the use of educating girls, men argued, when their role in life was merely to marry, have children, and raise them? Advanced education simply wasn't necessary.

Several women had different beliefs concerning women and education. One

Mary Lyons, founder of Mount Holyoke College.

Mount Holyoke College in South Hadley, Massachusetts, is the oldest women's college in the United States.

was Emma Willard. Born in Berlin, Connecticut, she was fortunate in having a father who wanted the best education possible for his daughter. Emma was particularly fond of solving mathematical problems, but she was saddened to discover that there was no opportunity for women to study advanced mathematics because women's brains were not considered equal to the task.

After she married John Willard, the head of an academy for boys in Middlebury, Vermont, she helped to establish a girls' boarding school there. In 1819, Willard asked the New York state legislature to fund an institution of higher learning for women. Although the governor supported the idea, the legislature balked.

Willard then raised the money from the citizens of Troy, New York. In 1821, the Troy Female Seminary became the first institution of higher learning for girls and, eventually, a model training school for teachers.

Willard offered her students courses in literature, science, social studies, and mathematics. Her most daring move was to teach physiology, the study of the human body, considered a delicate subject for young women of the time. When mothers of the girls visited the

Catherine Beecher devoted her energies toward schooling young girls to be teachers.

Harriet Beecher Stowe's <u>Uncle Tom's Cabin</u> *made a powerful statement against slavery.*

classroom, they were shocked to see a student drawing a heart, arteries, and veins on the blackboard while explaining the body's circulatory system. Afterward, they prevailed upon Willard to paste heavy paper over the pages in the girls' textbooks that depicted the human body.

By 1830, the enrollment of students at the school had reached approximately 300. Willard remained its head until 1838.

By 1872, over 12,000 women had attended the school. Many of its graduates established their own female academies. The institution later became famous as the Emma Willard School, the name by which it is known today.

The training of women teachers was also the concern of Catherine Beecher, a sister of Harriet Beecher Stowe, author of *Uncle Tom's Cabin*. Catherine Beecher operated a successful seminary for girls in Hartford, Connecticut, from 1823 to 1827. She later devoted most of her considerable energies toward establishing teacher-training schools in midwestern cities. She was particularly suc-

cessful in Milwaukee, Wisconsin, founding the Milwaukee Normal Institute and High School in 1850.

The institution was renamed Milwaukee Female College in 1853 and, later, simply, Milwaukee College. It is now a branch of the University of Wisconsin.

Mary Lyon's contribution was Mount Holyoke Female Seminary, a school for girls, "based entirely on Christian principles," that she founded in South Hadley, Massachusetts, in 1837. Today it is Mount Holyoke College.

In her appeal to women for funds, Lyon declared "this work of supplying teachers is a great work, and it must be done, or our country is lost, and the world will remain unconverted." Mount Holyoke is the oldest women's college in the United States.

Emma Willard, Catherine Beecher, and Mary Lyon did more than provide young women with the opportunities for secondary schooling to learn teaching skills. They also provided the knowledge and understanding that helped young women to begin to question their role in society.

For women of the 1800s who wanted or needed to work, teaching was the most attractive job available. Here a teacher poses with her class outside their Oklahoma Territory sod schoolhouse in 1895.

Factory Women

For women of the early 1800s who wanted to work, teaching was the most attractive job available. Women were also employed as household servants. But, normally, single white women did not seek jobs as domestics. These were filled by new immigrants or free black women.

By the 1820s, women in the Northeast had another choice. In 1814, the first power-driven loom for weaving had gone into operation in Waltham, a small Massachusetts town near Boston. Three more power looms were operating in Fall River by 1817. It wasn't long before textile mills began to spring up throughout New England, wherever there were fast-flowing rivers to supply the power.

For their labor supply, mill owners could not call upon young men, for they were needed on the farms. And married women had children to care for. The mill owners turned to the young unmarried women of New England, who were already skilled in spinning and weaving at home.

The owners promised good wages, pleasant working conditions, and cheery company-run boardinghouses, where the young women would live.

At first, the young women looked upon mill work as an adventure, a chance to leave home and become independent. They considered such work only temporary, something to do for a few years before they married.

But life for the mill girls proved difficult. In Lowell, Fall River, Waltham, and other mill towns, girls worked a six-day week. They had to be on the job by five o'clock in the morning. Except for a half-hour break for breakfast and one for dinner, they worked until sunset.

The mills were hot in the summer, cold in the winter, and filled with smelly air. The work was exhausting, and wages were low. There was no privacy in the company-run boardinghouses. The girls often slept six to a room, two to a bed. They had to abide by a ten o'clock curfew.

In time, mill girls learned to band together to seek to improve working conditions. In 1828, 400 women workers in a Dover, New Hampshire, mill walked off their jobs to protest fines the owner assessed for lateness. This was the first strike by women factory workers in America.

In 1834, women went on strike in

Women shoemakers on strike in Lynn, Massachusetts, in 1860.

The weave room of a Fall River, Massachusetts, cotton mill.

This is how "the school mistress" was portrayed in an 1853 book titled <u>Western Characters</u>.

Lowell when wages were cut. In 1836, they struck a second time when boardinghouse fees were raised without any increase in wages. Some 1,500 workers marched through Lowell singing:

> *Oh, isn't it a pity, such a pretty girl*
>   *as I*
> *Should be sent into a factory to*
>   *pine away and die?*
> *Oh, I cannot be a slave*
> *Oh, I will not be a slave*
> *For I'm so fond of liberty*
> *I cannot be a slave.*

The mill workers in New England blazed the trail. In the years that followed, workers in other industries organized to protest low-paying jobs or hazardous working conditions.

None of the early protests or strikes achieved any immediate benefits because the mill owners were too powerful. Nevertheless, the workers of Lowell and other communities introduced the concepts of labor organization and political action, which would be powerful weapons in years to come.

Lucretia Mott was active both as an abolitionist and as an advocate of women's rights.

Anti-Slavery Women

A gentle, self-confident woman with a soft voice, Lucretia Mott was one of the most noted female abolitionists. Born in 1793 on the island of Nantucket off Cape Cod, as a teenager she taught school near Poughkeepsie, New York. Through that experience, she learned firsthand that women received much less pay than men for doing the same work.

At 28, living in Philadelphia, she was ordained as a Quaker minister, and became active in the anti-slavery movement. She founded the Female Anti-Slavery Society and, in 1837, helped organize the Anti-Slavery Convention of American Women.

As abolitionists, women like Lucretia

Mott learned a wide range of tactics that they would later use in their fight for their own rights. They learned how to lecture and petition, and how to organize and raise funds. They also gained experience in resisting male objections and attacks. They would later use these tactics in their struggle to gain voting rights, fair wages, and a larger role outside the home.

When the World Anti-Slavery Convention was called into session in London in 1840, Lucretia Mott and many other female anti-slavery leaders crossed the Atlantic to attend. They were shocked and humiliated when the men who controlled the convention voted to exclude women from taking part. They could only be observers, the men said. When the women showed up at the convention hall, they were made to sit in the gallery, separated by a curtain from the main delegation.

Also attending the convention was Elizabeth Cady Stanton, who was to become a leader of the first women's movement in the United States. Twenty-five years old at the time and a graduate of Emma Willard's academy for women, Stanton's interest in

The Executive Committee of the Philadelphia Anti-Slavery Society in 1851, with Lucretia Mott seated in the first row.

Elizabeth Cady Stanton was a driving force for women's rights for more than half a century.

women's rights had begun as a child. Her father had been a lawyer, and on visits to his office she had seen firsthand how the law worked to deny women their property rights. She married Henry B. Stanton, an abolitionist in 1840, the same year she went to the Anti-Slavery Convention in London.

Many years later, Stanton recalled the convention, her conversations with Lucretia Mott, and their determination to start an organization that would be concerned with equality for women. "The acquaintance of Lucretia Mott, who was a broad, liberal thinker in politics, religion, and all questions of reform, opened to me a new world of thought," Stanton wrote in her memoirs, published in 1898.

The two women walked about London to see the sights. Said Stanton: "As Mrs. Mott and I walked home, arm in arm, commenting on the incidents of the day, we resolved to hold a convention as soon as we returned home, and form a society to advance the rights of women."

Eight years were to pass, however, before Stanton and Mott were able to call the convention into session.

Pioneers for Women's Rights

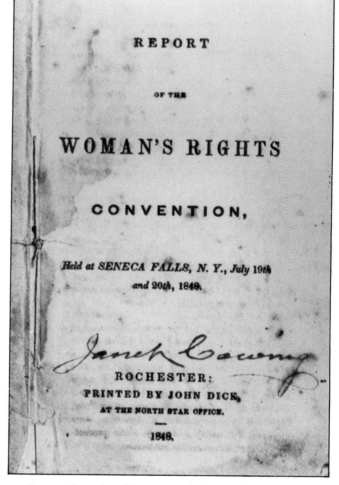

REPORT

OF THE

WOMAN'S RIGHTS

CONVENTION,

Held at SENECA FALLS, N. Y., July 19th
and 20th, 1848.

ROCHESTER:
PRINTED BY JOHN DICK,
AT THE NORTH STAR OFFICE.
—
1848.

Cover for the "Report of the Woman's Rights Convention."

The almost century-long struggle on the part of women to win the vote had its beginnings in Seneca Falls, a small manufacturing town in western New York State. It was there that Elizabeth Cady Stanton, her husband, and their children moved in 1847.

In Boston, where the family had first lived, Stanton had kept busy attending lectures and conferences concerning social issues. She also enjoyed concerts and the theater. But Seneca Falls, a very small town, was a disaster for her. Her husband was often away on business, and she felt isolated, lonely, and overworked.

Eight years had passed since she and Lucretia Mott had attended the World Anti-Slavery Convention in London and had talked about organizing a convention of women. In the summer of 1848, the two women met at a tea party in Waterloo, New York, near Seneca Falls. Women's rights was what they talked about.

Their discussion led to the publication

Frederick Douglass (here with his grandson Joseph), well-known as one of the first African-American abolitionists, supported Elizabeth Cady Stanton in her efforts to gain voting rights for women.

of an announcement in the *Seneca County Courier* on July 14, 1848, that called upon all interested parties to attend a convention to discuss the social, civil, and religious rights of women. The convention was to be held the following week at the Wesleyan Chapel in Seneca Falls.

Some 300 people arrived in Seneca Falls to attend the meeting, scheduled for July 19 and 20. Stanton had wanted the meeting to be for women exclusively, but when approximately 40 men showed up she decided they should be included.

There were several speeches, and then Stanton read the Declaration of Sentiments, which she had modeled after the Declaration of Independence. It declared, "We hold these truths to be self-evident: that all men and women are created equal; that they are endowed by their Creator with certain inalienable rights; that among these are life, liberty, and the pursuit of happiness . . ."

Then the declaration listed the injustices that women were being made to suffer. This section was followed by 12 resolutions, which included demands that women be given rights to own property, exercise free speech, and control their wages.

Stanton shocked the convention with one additional resolution — that women be granted the right to vote. Even Lucretia Mott got nervous. "We must go slowly," she warned Stanton.

But Frederick Douglass, a former slave and one of the most famous African-American abolitionists, came forward to support Stanton's bold proposal. The resolution was passed by the convention, but by a small margin.

Today, Seneca Falls is often looked upon as the birthplace of the American feminist movement. Two weeks after the meeting, a second convention was held in Rochester, New York. Others followed in small towns and large cities in Ohio, Massachusetts, Pennsylvania, and Indiana. No longer were women's rights merely a concept, an idea. Now they were a clear-cut goal, which many women believed could be achieved by working together.

"Failure is Impossible!"

Lucy Stone was the star speaker in the women's fight for equal rights.

Three women played vital leadership roles in the women's rights movement for more than half a century. Elizabeth Cady Stanton imparted calm wisdom; she was a thinker, a writer. Lucy Stone was its greatest orator. Susan B. Anthony was the movement's chief organizer, providing both force and direction.

Small and slight, with a beautiful, clear, and musical voice, Lucy Stone was one of the first women to make women's rights her number one priority. As a young girl growing up in a struggling farm family in western Massachusetts, she made up her mind she would not end up an overworked wife like her mother. She begged her father to let her stay in school until she could become a teacher and support herself. She eventually saved enough money to attend Oberlin College, the only college in the nation to admit women and blacks.

As the women's movement was being launched, Stone was its star speaker. Elizabeth Cady Stanton described her as "the first woman who really stirred the nation's heart on the subject of women's wrongs."

Stone detested the laws that prevented women from owning property and controlling their earnings. A married woman was virtually her husband's possession.

In traveling the country to lecture,

Susan B. Anthony was called the "Napoleon" of the women's movement.

Stone met Henry Blackwell, a successful businessman and dedicated abolitionist, who won her respect and love. Although she had said she would never marry, Stone accepted Blackwell once he promised her a marriage of equality. At their wedding ceremony in 1855, the word "obey" was removed from their marriage vows and the couple read a protest against traditional marriage laws.

Stone, who firmly believed a woman should maintain her own identity, kept

On November 8, 1892, election day, Lucy Stone wrote, "The consent of the governed woman is as necessary to a _just_ government as is the consent of the governed man."

her own last name after the marriage. In the years that followed, other women who decided not to change their names after marrying came to be known as "Lucy Stoners."

Susan B. Anthony was born in Adams, Massachusetts, in 1820 and raised a Quaker by a father who believed in the equality of men and women. He saw to it that his daughters as well as his sons were well educated.

After teaching school for ten years, Anthony, in 1849, joined the temperance movement, which campaigned to prohibit alcohol. Most temperance groups of the time permitted women to play only a limited role. In 1852, when Anthony attended a temperance rally in Albany, New York, she was not permitted to speak because she was a woman. "The sisters were not invited here to speak," said the chairman, "but to listen and learn." Anthony then formed a separate Woman's State Temperance Society. Men were permitted to speak at meetings but not to hold office.

Anthony was also active in the anti-slavery movement. In 1851 she went to Seneca Falls to attend an anti-slavery meeting. There she met Elizabeth Cady Stanton. It was the beginning of a life-long friendship. Much of Anthony's

writing, lecturing, and organizing was accomplished in partnership with Stanton. At her Seneca Falls home, it was said, Stanton "forged the thunderbolts" that Anthony "fired" into the world.

Besides her work on behalf of the anti-slavery movement, Anthony campaigned for equal pay for women. She believed that as long as women were exploited as cheap labor, they would be given only poor-paying, low-status jobs.

Women's property rights — or lack of them — was another of her concerns. In New York, state legislators looked upon women's rights as a joke. Anthony traveled throughout the state, speaking

Susan B. Anthony's profile appears on $1 coins minted in 1979 and 1980. She is the first woman to be pictured on a U.S. coin in general circulation.

out and collecting signatures by the thousands. In 1866, the state of New York finally passed the Married Women's Property Act. Women still could not vote and they still were not equal to men under the law, but by virtue of the new legislation they gained some rights to property and wages.

In the year following the Civil War, Anthony and Stanton worked as a team on behalf of women's sufferage — the right to vote. Today, Anthony ranks as one of the most honored of all American feminists. After her death in 1906, women continued to be inspired by her rallying cry, "Failure is impossible!"

The bloomer costume featured a knee-length skirt over baggy pantaloons.

This was called an "extreme" version of Elizabeth Smith Miller's fashion innovation.

Dress Reform

Women faced strong resistance when they spoke out and called for change. When they actually did change themselves, rejecting the long and heavy skirts and tight corsets that were the custom of the time, in favor of more sensible clothing, the public did not merely take a stand against the innovation; women found themselves the victims of public ridicule.

Gerrit Smith, a noted abolitionist and a supporter of women's rights, declared that women could not hope to be accepted by men as equals until they began to dress more practically. That meant abandoning heavy, trailing skirts and the long corsets worn beneath them. The corsets were sometimes laced so tightly that they made breathing difficult.

Elizabeth Smith Miller, Gerrit Smith's daughter, was the first to try something new. Her costume consisted of a pair of ballooning trousers worn underneath a knee-length skirt. Her cousin, Elizabeth Cady Stanton, was so impressed by the "incredible freedom" of the new style that she made herself a similar costume. Other reformers, including Lucy Stone and the Grimké sisters, tried the new outfit, too.

Amelia Bloomer was yet another feminist who adopted the pantaloon-type costume. A temperance reformer and advocate of women's rights, Bloomer published a journal, *The Lily*, and in its pages she supported the new style. The first article appeared in 1851. Hundreds of women wrote to her, asking for sewing instructions. Bloomer responded by publishing pictures and patterns.

Because Bloomer became closely identified with the new style, people started calling it the "bloomer costume," "bloomerettes," and, eventually, "bloomers."

The women who wore bloomers could not have been prepared for the great

Amelia Bloomer, wearing the practical style of dress she favored.

wave of hostility that swamped them. Newspapers and magazines ridiculed the costume. Men made fun of it. Little boys hooted at bloomer-wearing women. Nothing else the feminists of the 1850s said or did attracted so much attention.

Elizabeth Cady Stanton could not even win over her own family. Her father wrote that "no woman of good sense and delicacy" would "make a guy of herself." He hoped that when Elizabeth came to visit she would not be wearing bloomers. Her sister wept when she heard the news. And her two sons, away at boarding school, let their mother know that they did not want her to wear the "short dress" when she came to see them.

The jeers and hateful comments continued without letup. The reformers realized that their arguments for women's rights were being blotted out by the frenzy over fashion. Although they found that bloomers made their lives more comfortable and enabled them to move about with greater ease, the women who had been fearless enough to try the costume gave up the experiment in less than three years.

The Civil War

With the outbreak of the Civil War in 1861, women's efforts on behalf of equal rights came to a standstill. Yet through a wide range of activities that were spawned during the war, which lasted four long years, women gained organizational experience and a new public voice that would help them in achieving their own goals.

In the North, Dr. Elizabeth Blackwell, the first woman in the United States to receive a medical degree, pioneered in the training of Army nurses. Her work led to the formation of the Sanitary Commission, which played a vital role in the war effort. It recruited nurses for hospitals, provided medicine, bandages, and even food, and fought for improved sanitation at army camps.

The Sanitary Commission expanded into an enormous and complex relief organization, supported by approximately 7,000 local societies. Thousands of civic-minded women, the first organized "volunteers," also collected food and clothing and distributed it to the needy. The organization raised and spent more than $15,000,000 for supplies during the war, a huge sum for the time.

In the South, nurses toiled with the same dedication. Many cared for the sick and wounded in their own homes.

During the war, women also took jobs left vacant by men. For the first time, women were hired in government offices. In Columbia, South Carolina, for

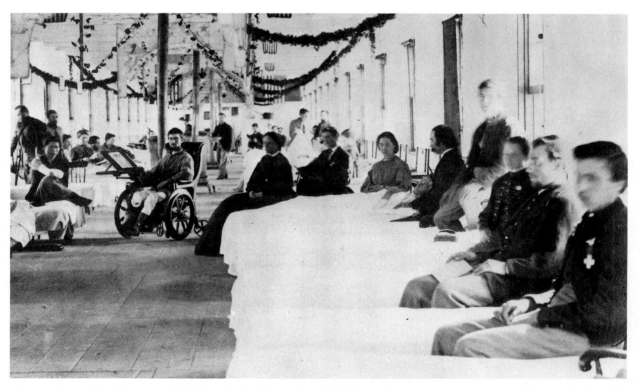

A ward in a Washington, DC, hospital during the Civil War. Two women are seated by the bed to the right, surrounded by wounded men.

28

example, more than 200 women worked for the Confederate Treasury Note Bureau.

Women also were hired by munitions plants and government arsenals, where they often worked with hazardous chemicals. Thousands of women went to work in textile mills.

Elizabeth Cady Stanton and Susan B. Anthony, like most other abolitionists, were wary of President Abraham Lincoln. They opposed any plan to settle differences with the slave states through compromise.

Stanton and Anthony believed that women should have a voice in settling

In 1860, when she was only 18, Anna Dickinson was speaking out on behalf of abolition and women's rights.

the important issues of the day. They wrote: "In nursing the sick and wounded, knitting socks, and making jellies, the bravest and best may weary

if the thoughts mount not to some noble purpose . . ."

Above all things — Liberty

Anna E. Dickinson

9.7.75.

In giving her autograph in 1875, Anna Dickinson added an eloquent inscription, "Above all things— Liberty."

The "noble purpose" cited by Stanton and Anthony was freedom for all slaves. Lincoln's Emancipation Proclamation, issued on January 1, 1863, promised freedom only to those slaves in the rebel states, but not to those in the Union slave-holding states of Maryland, Missouri, West Virginia, Tennessee, Kentucky, and Delaware.

Stanton and Anthony formed the National Women's Loyal League in May 1863, the goal of which was to goad Congress into passing the Thirteenth Amendment, which would prohibit slavery in Union as well as Confederate territory. For the next fifteen months, the two women worked tirelessly, gathering signatures in support of their cause. Their massive petition rolls containing nearly 400,000 signatures, some from as far away as California, were presented to Congress on February 9, 1864.

Among those feminists who spoke on behalf of the petition and the Loyal League was a brilliant and fiery young orator from Philadelphia named Anna

In 1864, Lillie Hitchcock Coit became one of the first female firefighters in the world.

Dickinson. She gave her first important speech in 1860, when she was 18. Abolition wasn't the only cause for which Dickinson campaigned. She also spoke on the "Rights and Wrongs of Women." Her career reached a high point on the evening of January 16, 1864, when she addressed an enormous gathering in the chamber of the House of Representatives.

During the Civil War, women proved their importance to the nation and once again demonstrated their political abilities. What women expected in return was that they would be granted the right to vote. It was women's natural right,

they said. No longer should that right be denied.

But powerful forces were leveled against them. Radical Republican Congressmen hoped that they could control the South by giving voting rights to black men, who would then vote Republican. Women's suffrage was of no importance to them.

Abolitionists, with whom Stanton, Anthony, and the other reformers had been closely allied, now refused to support women's suffrage. It was the "Negroes' turn," feminists were told. Nothing must be allowed to interfere. Women would have to wait.

Backward Steps

·····································

In the years following the ending of the Civil War in 1865, several Constitutional amendments were enacted on behalf of African-Americans. While the passage of these amendments represented a great leap forward, getting these new amendments to work was a different matter. It would be another century before the civil rights movement, led by Martin Luther King, Jr.,

Elizabeth Cady Stanton addresses the Senate Committee on Privileges and Elections. This engraving appeared in the New York Daily Graphic on January 16, 1878.

would force the federal government to fulfill the promises made after the Civil War.

The Thirteenth Amendment, which was ratified in 1865, made the Emancipation Proclamation law by prohibiting slavery in the United States. The Fourteenth Amendment, introduced in Congress in the summer of 1866, was intended to provide equality to all citizens. But it made specific references to "male inhabitants" and "male citizens" in the section dealing with the right to vote.

While the Fourteenth Amendment benefitted black Americans, it was a frustrating setback for the women's rights movement. Stanton and Anthony were horrified by the legislation. For the first time in history, the Constitution used the word "males" instead of speaking simply of "citizens" or "the people." The wording of the amendment raised the question as to whether women were full-fledged citizens of the United States anymore.

Feminists opposed the passage of the

The first black woman to speak out against slavery, Sojourner Truth also fought for women's rights.

Victoria Woodhull, one of the most colorful figures in the women's movement.

Autograph of

Victoria C. Woodhull,

Future Presidentess,

Date

Woodhull, who once sought the presidency, had an unusual name for the office.

amendment. They previously had been denied the vote on the basis of state law alone. With the Fourteenth Amendment, the Constitution itself had become a barrier. "If the word 'male' be inserted now," said Stanton, "it will take a century at least to get it out." Stanton was close to being right.

Sojourner Truth, a former slave and the first black woman to speak out against slavery, agreed with Anthony, Stanton, and the other feminists. "There is a great stir about colored men getting their rights, but not a word about colored women," she said, "and if colored men get their rights and not colored women theirs, you see, colored men will be the masters over women.

" . . . I wish woman to have her voice."

Despite the opposition, the Fourteenth Amendment was ratified in 1868. The following year, Anthony, with Stanton, founded the National Woman Suffrage Association (NWSA), which championed a broad range of issues important to women, suffrage being foremost.

The Fourteenth Amendment was followed in 1870 by the Fifteenth, which reads: "The right of citizens of the United States to vote shall not be denied or abridged by the United States or by any State, on account of race, color, or previous condition of servitude."

Feminists realized it would have been very easy for Congress to have included the word "sex" in the amendment, which would have granted women voting rights. The fact that Congress hadn't, made them realize that women's suffrage was still a long way from becoming a reality.

During this period, other women were active on other fronts. In 1871, Victoria Woodhull, a spirited feminist and colorful orator, appeared before the House Judiciary Committee in Washington, DC, to speak on the subject of women's suffrage. Susan B. Anthony was so pleased with what Woodhull had done that she invited her to make a major speech at the 1871 convention of the NWSA.

The following year, the brash Woodhull tried to take over the NWSA to advance her own political ambitions. After Anthony crushed Woodhull's move, Woodhull and her supporters formed their own political party, then held a convention and named Woodhull as the party's presidential candidate. But on election day she was in jail, charged with sending obscene materials through the mail.

Belva Lockwood, a leader in the suffrage movement, and one of the few women lawyers of the 1870s, also had the presidency in mind. After being admitted to the bar in Washington, DC, in 1873, Lockwood was refused the right to try cases before the U.S. Supreme Court. Unwilling to accept the ruling, she eventually won passage of a bill that enabled women to plead cases before the Court. President Rutherford B. Hayes signed the bill into law in 1879.

Lockwood ran for president in 1884 as the candidate of the National Equal Rights Party. Campaigning on a platform that called for equal rights for women and a standardization of marriage and divorce laws, Lockwood received 4,149 votes (out of the approximately ten million votes cast) in six states. She believed she was defrauded of many more. Lockwood was the first woman in American history to receive votes in a presidential election.

Belva Lockwood, reformer and suffragist leader, and, in 1884, the first woman to receive votes in a presidential election.

The territory of Wyoming granted women the right to vote in 1869. This engraving records the scene when women cast their ballots in the city of Cheyenne.

Victories in the West

In 1869, the same year that Susan B. Anthony and Elizabeth Cady Stanton founded the National Woman Suffrage Association, the territory of Wyoming gave women the right to vote. The women of Wyoming thus became the only women in the world legally permitted to cast ballots in government elections.

Women won the vote in Wyoming without the help of Anthony, Stanton, or the organized suffrage movement. Women's suffrage was looked upon as something of a necessity there.

Wyoming in the 1860s was rough, rugged, and sparsely settled. The big-

A follower of Susan B. Anthony's, Esther Morris pushed for voting rights in Wyoming.

gest settlement was South Pass City, a community of 2,000, where gold deposits had been found in 1867. Today it is a ghost town.

Permanent settlers in Wyoming were outnumbered by gold seekers, gamblers, cowboys, pioneers on their way to Oregon and California, and thousands of railroad workers who were laying tracks for the transcontinental railroad.

Community leaders and legislators had their hands full trying to control the rowdy population and attract permanent settlers to the territory. Esther Morris, from Oswego, New York, who had settled in Wyoming with her husband and their three sons in 1869, had the answer. A follower of Susan B. Anthony, Morris urged lawmakers to pass a bill for women's suffrage, pointing out that in so doing they would increase the voting strength of law-abiding citizens. She said that women's suffrage would "prove a great advertisement" and draw many more families to the territory.

The legislators passed a women's suffrage bill without delay. When the governor signed it, Wyoming women became the first in the United States with the right to vote.

By 1915, as this flyer indicates, twelve Western states (actually, eleven states plus the Territory of Alaska) had granted voting rights to women.

The election of 1870, the first in which the women of Wyoming took part, was observed to be more calm and orderly than previous elections. There was far less brawling and drunkeness. "It seemed more like a Sunday than an election day," noted Stanton and Anthony in their *History of Woman Suffrage*.

When Wyoming applied for statehood in 1890, many members of the U.S. House of Representatives opposed women's suffrage. They were reluctant to see Wyoming join the Union. But the Wyoming legislators had no intention of repealing the voting rights law. The legislators sent a message to Congress that read: "We may stay out of the Union for 100 years, but we will come in with our women." Wyoming was voted into the Union, but by a slim margin.

Colorado, in 1893, became the second state to grant women's suffrage. Utah, which became a state in 1896 under a constitution that granted voting rights to women, was the third. Idaho also enfranchised women in 1896. Several other western states followed in turn, but almost two decades passed before women in any of the eastern states were able to vote.

Frances Willard, leader of the temperance movement, was also an activist for suffrage.

Women and Reform

After the Civil War, Susan B. Anthony and Elizabeth Cady Stanton became close allies, and through the National Woman Suffrage Association continued to fight for voting rights on local, state, national, and even international levels. The two women also continued to work for property rights for married women and equal pay for working women.

Lucy Stone and her husband, Henry Blackwell, and an army of women concentrated on winning suffrage not by constitutional amendment, but on a state-by-state basis. These women started the American Woman Suffrage Association (AWSA). This split in the women's ranks was to last for 20 years.

At the same time, a new group of women's leaders began to capture public attention. These women sought to solve a serious social problem of the day — alcoholism. While men were much more likely to be heavy drinkers, it was the women who often suffered the most, for the law placed married women at the mercy of their husbands.

In a temperance crusade in 1873, tens of thousands of women took to the streets of small midwestern towns, praying, singing, and bursting into saloons to close them by the thousands. Out of these protest movements came the Woman's Christian Temperance Union (WCTU), organized in Cleveland, Ohio, in 1874, which was to become the largest and most influential women's organization of its day.

The WCTU grew by leaps and bounds after Frances Willard, a noted educator, became its president in 1879. With 10,000 local branches in every state in the union, the WCTU claimed to speak for more than 200,000 women. Willard divided the organization, which she called "the great society," into 40 departments, each headed by a woman.

While Willard was indeed concerned about protecting women from drunken husbands, she also steered the WCTU toward the support of suffrage and happily poured money into suffrage campaigns. She believed that women could not protect their homes and families from the evil effects of alcohol unless they had a voice in public affairs.

Willard was interested in any cause that would help women and children. Through the WCTU, she campaigned

In 1885, would-be women voters stormed a New York polling place.

Work of the Woman's Christian Temperance Union led to the passage of the Eighteenth Amendment, which banned the manufacture and sale of alcoholic beverages. Here authorities in Philadelphia destroy barrels of illegal beer.

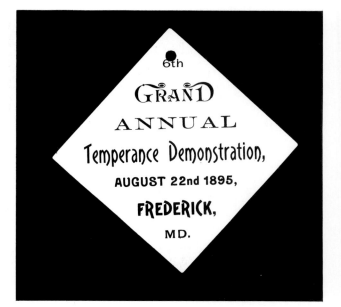

6th
GRAND ANNUAL
Temperance Demonstration,
AUGUST 22nd 1895,
FREDERICK,
MD.

In Frederick, Maryland, temperance demonstrations were held annually.

for kindergartens, prison reform, child labor laws, and laws to protect working women. "Do Everything" became the WCTU's motto.

After Willard's death in 1898, the WCTU changed in character. Its goals became more limited, as its leaders concentrated on the temperance movement almost exclusively. Working closely with churches, schools, and reform groups, the WCTU was eventually successful in winning the passage of the Eighteenth Amendment to the Constitution, which prohibited the manufacture, sale, and import of alcoholic beverages. The amendment was in force from 1920 until 1933.

But through its campaign for temperance, the WCTU was harmful to the suffrage cause. Many men opposed women getting the right to vote because they had become convinced that they would use the ballot box to ban the sale of alcoholic beverages. Companies that sold and distributed beer, wine, and liquor felt the same way, and campaigned against women's suffrage for half a century.

The WCTU is active to this day. With its national headquarters in Evanston, Illinois, the organization has as one of its chief goals the education of young people as to the harmful effects of alcohol and other narcotic substances.

Women, by tradition, had no problem finding work as nurses.

Working Women

At the beginning of the 1900s, women started to become more involved in business, industry, and the professions. In 1890, there were about 4,000,000 women employed outside the home. By 1900, the number had risen to 5,300,000, and by 1910, to 7,400,000.

The biggest percentage of working women were still those employed in private homes as maids, cooks, and laundresses. Large numbers of women were also employed as farm laborers, teachers, nurses, and salesclerks.

The invention of the typewriter, produced in huge quantities during the 1870s, revolutionized office work.

Office work had become a fast growing field for women. Before the Civil War, office clerks had almost always been men, and the clerical jobs they held were looked upon as a gateway to success in the business world. Few offices employed women. In 1870, in fact, there were only seven women stenographers in the nation.

By 1900, there were 200,000 women officer workers and, by 1930, some 2,000,000. The typewriter, first produced in large quantities during the 1870s, helped to cause the revolution. The operation of the typewriter was looked upon as women's work. When other office machines were invented, women were employed to run them — as bookkeepers, stenographers, and cashiers. But no longer did clerical jobs lead naturally to management positions.

When it came to factory work, great numbers of women were employed in the garment trades. These factories,

During the early 1900s, children by the tens of thousands worked in Northern mills and factories. This girl, a spinner in a Vermont cotton mill, claimed to be 12 years old, but her co-worker said she was 10.

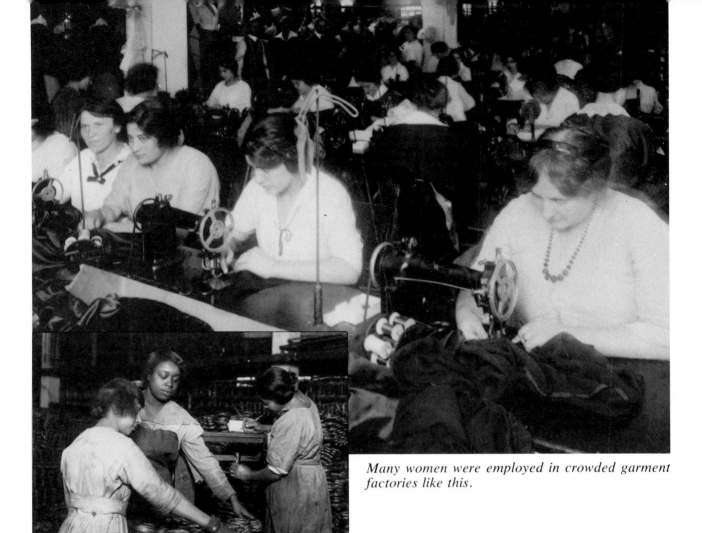

Many women were employed in crowded garment factories like this.

Thousands of jobs for women opened in heavy industry during World War I.

often called "sweatshops," were usually housed in lofts in old buildings that were crowded, smelly, dimly lit, cold in the winter, and stifling in the summer.

Women factory workers were drawn from the great flood of immigrants from eastern and southern Europe that came to the United States beginning in the 1880s. They joined the Irish, Germans, and Scandinavians who had immigrated earlier in the century. Often paid by the piece rather than receiving a fixed weekly wage, women factory workers toiled from ten to twelve hours a day. When a woman became highly skilled

and began to produce a decent income, her employer was likely to reduce her piece rate.

Children also worked in sweatshops, tens of thousands of them employed in northern mills. In 1912, the platform of the Progressive party called for labor reforms that included an eight-hour day, a six-day workweek, and an end to child labor under the age of 16.

As industrial workers, women were offered only low-paying unskilled jobs. This situation changed in 1917 when America entered World War I. When men enlisted or were drafted into the military, women were called upon to take their place in the labor force. Women worked in factories assembling electrical appliances, airplane and automobile parts, machine tools, and explosives. They drove trucks, operated trolley cars, and delivered milk, coal, and ice.

Some women also played an active role in the war, in which well over a million American men were rushed to France to help the British and French defeat Germany. Women faced bullets and shells as nurses, couriers, and ambulance drivers.

The number of women who took jobs in heavy industry during World War I was small in comparison with the number of women who would do so during World War II in the 1940s. Yet they successfully challenged the idea that women were capable of performing only limited kinds of work.

The impact they had was slight, however. After the war, when men were discharged from the armed forces, women were forced to give up their good-paying, highly skilled industrial jobs and return to their traditional forms of work.

American Army nurses parade in Paris in 1918 in celebration of the Fourth of July.

Women enlist in the U.S. Navy in World War I.

Toward an Equal Education

Prudence Crandall, a Quaker, ran a successful school for young ladies from well-to-do families in Canterbury, Connecticut, in 1833–34. She had as a servant a free Negro woman who prevailed upon her to accept a Negro girl, Sarah Harris, as one of her pupils. The townspeople boiled with rage and demanded the student be dismissed at once. Rather than turn Sarah Harris away, Crandall closed the school.

Founded in 1881, Spelman College is the nation's oldest four-year liberal arts college for black women.

Mary McLeod Bethune was the founder of Bethune-Cookman College.

That was not the end of it. Several weeks after closing the first school, Crandall opened another, with seventeen Negro students. When town officials were unable to shut down the school by legal means, other methods were tried. School windows were broken. Teachers and pupils were stoned. Shopkeepers refused to sell food to the school. Doctors withheld their services. Crandall held out for a year and a half. But after a night during which men pounded the school's front door and walls with battering rams, Crandall, saying that she feared for the lives of her students, announced the school would be closed.

Black girls seeking an education found their opportunities severely limited by racism. In many cases, they turned to women — mostly black, but some white — for their schooling.

In 1886, Lucy C. Lainey founded Haines Normal Institute in Augusta,

Georgia. She started with 75 pupils. By 1940, enrollment had passed one thousand. After later merging with the A. R. Johnson High School, it became Lucy C. Lainey High School, the name by which it is known today.

Charlotte Hawkins Brown's contribution was the Palmer Memorial Institute in Sedalia, North Carolina, which she established in 1902. It became one of the leading schools for black girls in the South. Nannie Burroughs, using the slogan "We Specialize in the Wholly Impossible," founded the National Training School for Girls in Washington, DC.

In the spring of 1881, two teachers, Sophia Packard and Harriet E. Giles, arrived in Atlanta from Massachusetts to start the Atlanta Baptist Female Seminary. With the support of local ministers, they opened their school that same year in the basement of the Friendship Baptist Church. They had one hundred dollars, 11 students, a Bible, a pad, and a pencil. Today it is Spelman College, the nation's oldest four-year liberal arts institution of higher learning for black women. The school now boasts an enrollment of approximately 1,700 and a reputation for high academic standards and notable achievements on the part of its alumnae.

In Daytona Beach, Florida, in 1904,

In 1923, the school Bethune founded merged with Darnell-Cookman Institute to become Bethune-Cookman College.

Mary McLeod Bethune with a group of Bethune-Cookman students in 1943.

Mary McLeod Bethune, born on a plantation where she later picked cotton, started a school in the home of the Williams family on Oak Street. Her son and five girls were her first students. They earned money for beds, books, and groceries by baking sweet-potato pies and selling them to railroad workers.

In 1923, the school merged with Darnell-Cookman Institute of Jacksonville, Florida. It became Bethune-Cookman College in 1932. Today, Bethune-Cookman, a coeducational liberal arts college with some 2,300 students (62 percent of whom are female) is known for its quality educational programs. It stands as a monument to Mary McLeod Bethune's dedication, enthusiasm, and organizational skills. In 1936, President Franklin D. Roosevelt named Bethune to the post of Negro Affairs Director for the National Youth Administration.

Bethune was founder of the National Council of Negro Women and a force in many other professional and civic organizations. In 1941, at the age of 66, she refused to take her doctor's advice to slow down. "For I am my mother's daughter," she wrote, "and the drums of Africa still beat in my heart. They will not let me rest while there is a single Negro boy or girl without a chance to prove his worth."

Emmeline Pankhurst, a British suffragist, is arrested outside Buckingham Palace in 1914. American feminists adopted militant tactics used by British women.

As President of the National American Woman Suffrage Association, Carrie Chapman Catt planned strategy that led to the passage of the Nineteenth Amendment.

Votes for Women

During the early 1900s, a new generation of feminists launched a final push for women's suffrage. Their efforts led eventually to the passage of the Nineteenth Amendment to the Constitution in 1920, giving women voting rights equal to men.

These women were inspired at least in part by what was happening in state legislatures in the West. Between 1910 and 1914, the states of Washington, California, Oregon, Arizona, Kansas, Montana, Nevada, Illinois, and the territory of Alaska passed legislation granting women's suffrage.

Newspapers sometimes ridiculed women in their quest for equal rights. This cartoon appeared in the Louisville Times in 1923.

At the same time, dramatic changes were taking place on an organizational level. Susan B. Anthony had retired as president of the National American Woman Suffrage Association (which had come into existence out of a merger of the National Woman Suffrage Association and the American Woman Suffrage Association) and had been succeeded by Carrie Chapman Catt, who was widely hailed for her brilliance as a strategist and an organizer. Catt believed that in order to secure passage of a federal suffrage amendment, women would first have to win grass-roots support for their cause. As Catt was putting her plans into action, her husband became ill and died, and, in 1904, Catt was forced to retire.

Under pressure from the membership, Catt took over the presidency of NAWSA a second time in 1916. She immediately developed what she called her "Winning Plan," which was intended to win ratification of the suffrage amendment by 1920.

Meanwhile, other women were taking bolder action. Two Americans, Harriet Stanton Blatch, the daughter of Elizabeth Cady Stanton, and Alice Paul, were active in England with Emmeline Pankhurst and other British suffragettes, who did not hesitate to use extreme methods to achieve their goals. When Blatch and Paul returned to the United States, they applied what they had learned in England to the American suffrage movement.

Suffragists from New York City hiked to Washington, DC, to parade on March 3, 1913, the day before President Wilson's inauguration.

Blatch organized suffrage parades in New York City, the first outdoor demonstrations by American suffragists. Alice Paul was more militant. She also had a splendid sense of timing. On the day before President-elect Woodrow Wilson was to be inaugurated in 1913, Paul organized a parade of several thousand women in support of suffrage. When the newly elected president arrived in the capital for his inauguration, he wondered why the streets were empty and there was no crowd to greet him. "Where are the people?" he asked.

"They're off watching the women," he was told.

The parade was a great success. The Washington police were so overwhelmed by all the marchers, that troops had to be brought in from a nearby Army base to keep control.

During the 1916 presidential election, Paul and members of her Woman's party campaigned to defeat the Democrats and Wilson. Peace was a major issue in the campaign. Wilson campaigned with the slogan, "Vote for Wilson, he kept us out of war." Paul and her supporters answered, "Vote against Wilson, he

President Wilson, who opposed women getting the right to vote, casts his ballot in the election of 1914.

Jeannette Rankin of Montana, the first woman elected to Congress, introduced the suffrage amendment on the floor of the House of Representatives.

kept us out of suffrage." Wilson won the election in a close race.

After the United States entered World War I in 1917, Paul and the Women's party stepped up their campaign. They stood in silent vigil in front of the White House and outside President Wilson's Washington home. Their signs accused the president of terrible deceit in fighting a war that was supposed to guarantee democratic principals in foreign lands, while at the same time denying democratic rights to American women.

After the protesting and picketing had gone on for several months, police began making arrests. At first the women were released without being sentenced. When they returned to the picket line, they were arrested again. This time they were found guilty of blocking sidewalk traffic and given prison sentences.

In prison, many of the women joined in a hunger strike. The authorities tried to force-feed them. The public, horrified by this harsh treatment, pitied the poor women and began to look with sympathy upon the cause of suffrage. When Paul and the others were eventually released from prison, they were greeted as heroes.

The dramatic demonstrations staged by Alice Paul and the Women's party, combined with Carrie Chapman Catt's hard work to win rank and file support, paid off. On January 10, 1918, Jeannette Rankin of Montana, who, when elected to the House of Representatives in 1916, had become the first female member of Congress, introduced the suffrage amendment on the floor of the House. One congressman left his wife's deathbed — at her request — to vote for the amendment. Another congressman was brought in on a stretcher. The final vote was 274 in favor of the amendment, 136 opposed. The amendment had passed by one vote more than the two-thirds majority required.

It took another year and a half for the amendment to win passage in the Senate. In June 1919, the amendment was submitted to the states for ratification. On August 26, 1920, after Tennessee had delivered the last needed vote, the Nineteenth Amendment became a part of the Constitution.

In the years that followed the passage of the Nineteenth Amendment, the Women's party set a new goal — full equality for women under the law. The organization began campaigning for an Equal Rights Amendment to the Constitution. The struggle to win passage of *that* amendment continues to this day.

Sixty-sixth Congress of the United States of America;

At the First Session,

Begun and held at the City of Washington on Monday, the nineteenth day of May, one thousand nine hundred and nineteen.

JOINT RESOLUTION

Proposing an amendment to the Constitution extending the right of suffrage to women.

Resolved by the Senate and House of Representatives of the United States of America in Congress assembled (two-thirds of each House concurring therein), That the following article is proposed as an amendment to the Constitution, which shall be valid to all intents and purposes as part of the Constitution when ratified by the legislatures of three-fourths of the several States.

"ARTICLE ————.

"The right of citizens of the United States to vote shall not be denied or abridged by the United States or by any State on account of sex.

"Congress shall have power to enforce this article by appropriate legislation."

F. H. Gillett
Speaker of the House of Representatives.

Thos. R. Marshall
Vice President of the United States and President of the Senate.

The Nineteenth Amendment, ratified on August 26, 1920, gave nationwide suffrage to women.

Alice Paul, an activist for women's suffrage, toasts (with grape juice) the vote of Tennessee, which assured passage of the Nineteenth Amendment.

President Roosevelt, with his dog, Fala.

The Great Depression

It was a bleak period in the nation's history that began with the stock market crash in October 1929 and continued through the 1930s. The economy nose-dived and unemployment soared. It was called the Great Depression.

Working women saw their problems worsen. Women in food processing plants and garment and textile factories suffered heavy layoffs. Office workers and those in sales jobs held on during the early 1930s, but eventually they, too, joined the ranks of the unemployed. By the end of the Depression, more

55

Frances Perkins, Secretary of Labor in the Roosevelt administration, was the first woman cabinet member.

women than men were without jobs.

When Franklin D. Roosevelt became president in 1933, he announced a "New Deal" to help put the nation back to work. The federal government began to play a more aggressive role in regulating the economy and supplying the basic needs of citizens who were unable to care for themselves — the poor, the elderly, and the unemployed. Some New Deal programs, however, chiefly the National Recovery Administration, discriminated against women.

With social welfare in the forefront of American politics, women who had experience as social reformers began to take on key roles. None was more important than Eleanor Roosevelt, who used her status as First Lady to speak out on behalf of those lacking political power.

Already a well-established political figure at the time her husband became president, Mrs. Roosevelt used articles in women's magazines, her frequent radio shows, and her nationally distributed newspaper column, "My Day," to call attention to the problems of women, children, minorities, and the unemployed.

To get newspapers to treat women's issues more seriously, Mrs. Roosevelt held press conferences to which only female reporters were invited. To call attention to how unfairly unemployed women were being treated by government relief agencies, she held a White House Conference on the subject.

Just as Hillary Rodham Clinton later did after Bill Clinton became president in 1993, Mrs. Roosevelt urged her husband to appoint more women to government posts. Frances Perkins, a social reformer who supported a minimum wage, maximum working hours, and the abolition of child labor, was named Secretary of Labor, becoming the first woman cabinet member.

President Roosevelt appointed many other women to "first" positions, including Ruth Bryan Owen, who was named ambassador to Denmark. She thus became the first woman diplomat to represent the United States in a foreign country.

Mary McLeod Bethune was named by Roosevelt to be Negro Affairs Director for the National Youth Administration. She helped thousands acquire jobs in work projects and scholarships to

Because her husband was unable to walk, Eleanor Roosevelt often acted as his eyes and ears. One of the most active First Ladies, especially for her time, here she prepares to descend to the depths of a coal mine.

On January 30, 1936, Eleanor Roosevelt cuts Franklin Roosevelt's birthday cake, celebrating the President's fifty-fourth birthday.

college during the Depression. She also became recognized as the unofficial leader of the "Black Cabinet," the African-American officials in federal agencies to whom Roosevelt turned for advice.

During the 1930s, women managed to make some narrow gains within the organized labor movement. The International Ladies Garment Workers Union (ILGWU), in an enormous membership drive, brought blacks, Latinos, and Asians into the fold for the first time. Women were largely responsible for increasing the ILGWU's membership by 300 percent to 800,000 workers. Yet, of the 24 members on the union's executive board, only one was a woman.

Women were able to benefit somewhat from the protective labor legislation of the New Deal and the development of unions on an industry-wide basis. And individual women gained power and status within the Roosevelt administration. But by the end of the 1930s, 21 states had no minimum-wage laws for women. Women were still not equal to men in the labor force.

Members of the Women's Army Corps—WACs—stand for inspection following their arrival in England in 1945.

Women at War

The attack by Japanese planes on Pearl Harbor on the morning of December 7, 1941, plunged the United States into World War II, energizing the industrial power of the nation, which helped put a speedy end to the Great Depression. Suddenly, there were jobs everywhere.

As had happened during World War I, when men left their jobs in offices and factories to enter the armed services, women were hired to replace them.

Six million American women joined the labor force during the war. Some two million of these took jobs in heavy industry — in aircraft plants and shipyards, and in the steel, electrical, and automotive industries. Women riveted and welded, and operated drill presses and overhead cranes.

Another two million of these women went to work in offices. Female workers soon dominated that field as a result. A shortage of teachers forced many communities to lift their restrictions on the hiring of married women. Women quickly came to be a majority in the teaching field as well.

Women also worked at scores of jobs that were once held almost exclusively by males. They became auto mechanics, house painters, train conductors, lumberjacks, and truck and taxicab drivers.

Black women who wanted to work now had the chance to do so. Before the war, almost three fourths of black working women were domestics, and another 20 percent worked on farms. During the war, black working women found jobs in factories. They also began to be accepted in jobs that had previously been reserved for whites almost exclusively. These included jobs in the health-care and clerical fields.

When the armed services faced labor shortages, they, too, turned to the nation's women. During 1942 and 1943, a woman's branch was created in each of the armed services. They were the Army WACs (for *W*omen's *A*rmy *C*orps); the Navy WAVES (*W*omen *A*ppointed for *V*oluntary *E*mergency *S*ervice); the Coast Guard SPARS (from *S*emper *Par*atus, Latin for "Always Ready," the Coast Guard motto); and the Marine Corps Women's Reserve (MCWR). Close to 350,000

Women Marines at the Marine Corps Air Station, Quantico, Virginia, attach depth charges to bomb racks of Marine Corps fighters.

women served in these units.

World War II ended on August 15, 1945, called V-J Day, the day Japan accepted the surrender terms of the Allied nations. As men were discharged from the military services, women by the millions were fired to make room for the returning servicemen. Within two months after V-J Day, 800,000 workers, most of them women, lost their jobs in the aircraft industry. In the shipyards and automobile and electric fields, layoffs were just as high.

Society encouraged women to reject any thoughts of a career. Devoting oneself only to home and family was presented as the ideal.

While many women had no wish to remain in the labor force, many others had decided they wanted to continue working. But they found skilled industrial jobs were no longer open to them. In the auto industry, for example, the percentage of women in the workforce fell from 25 to 7.5 percent.

When women went looking for work, they were offered "female" jobs. These were jobs for file clerks, not office managers; salesclerks, not sales managers; bookkeepers, not accountants; keypunch operators, not computer programmers; teachers, not principals; and executive secretaries, not executives.

Women also faced discrimination in terms of what they were paid. In 1950, women earned, on average, 65 percent of what men earned. By 1960, the amount had fallen to 60 percent.

Few women questioned exactly why they had only limited opportunities in the workplace or why they were underpaid in the jobs that were available to them. Why bother? Careers were strictly secondary, they were told. After all, a woman's role was to be a wife and mother.

Women had demonstrated during World War II that they could do countless better-paying jobs that had once been assigned to men on an exclusive basis. But not until women started to question the traditional role that society had thrust upon them — and do something about it — would their status begin to change.

Women also made important contributions on the home front during the war. Here nurses and nurses' aides march up Broadway in New York City as part of a campaign to recruit 500,000 volunteer workers.

Rosa Parks is escorted up the steps of the Montgomery County courthouse for her trial in connection with the bus boycott in Montgomery, Alabama.

Fighting for Civil Rights

On her five-mile ride to school every morning, eight-year-old Linda Brown often wondered why her bus passed right by Sumner Elementary School, just four blocks from her home. When Linda's father tried to enroll her in Sumner for fourth grade, Topeka, Kansas, school officials said no. It was 1951. Linda was black and Sumner was all-white. Segregation still prevailed despite the legal and political efforts of African-American individuals and organizations to end it.

But change was on the way. On May 17, 1954, in the case of *Brown* v. *Topeka Board of Education*, the Supreme Court ruled that school segregation was unconstitutional. That momentous decision set the stage for the civil rights movement.

Many observers say the movement

began in Montgomery, Alabama, in December 1955. Rosa Parks, a seamstress and secretary for the local branch of the National Association for the Advancement of Colored People (NAACP), boarded a city bus and sat in the "colored" section at the back. When the bus became crowded, the driver demanded she give up her seat for a white person. Rosa Parks refused and was arrested.

For the next year, to protest segregation in public transportation, black citizens of Montgomery walked to work instead of riding buses. The success of the boycott gave confidence to those who believed similar protests could force other cities in the South to change their policies.

Thousands of black Americans, supported by many whites, marched and protested through most of the decade that followed, challenging racial discrimination. Students staged sit-ins at segregated restaurants in an attempt to be served. Fire hoses were turned on them and they were stoned and beaten. Civil rights organizations launched huge voter registration drives in an effort to thwart white racists who sought to deprive blacks of their right to vote. The Reverend Dr. Martin Luther King, Jr., preaching nonviolence and racial brotherhood, emerged as the leader of the movement.

African-American women played a vital role in the movement. Fannie Lou Hamer, from Ruleville, Mississippi, the twelfth of twenty children, was one of the most zealous activists. In 1962, the 45-year-old Hamer went to the local

Martin Luther King, Jr., leads a line of black demonstrators who attempted to march on city hall in Birmingham, Alabama, in 1963.

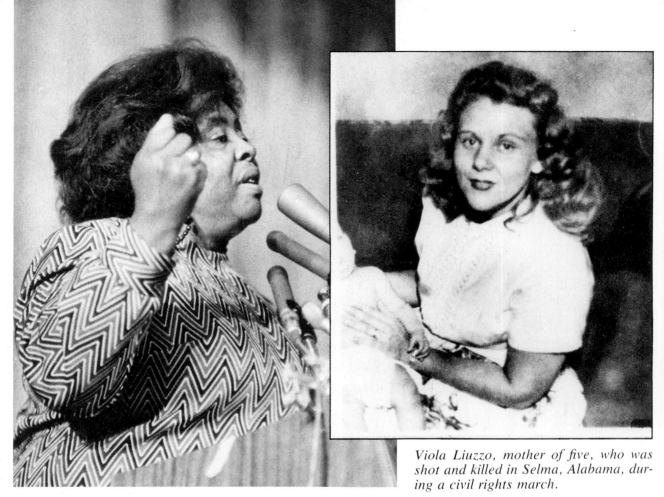

Viola Liuzzo, mother of five, who was shot and killed in Selma, Alabama, during a civil rights march.

Fannie Lou Hamer helped found the Freedom Democratic party, which challenged the all-white delegation from Mississippi at the 1964 Democratic National Convention.

courthouse to register to vote. Her employer had told her not to do so. Soon after, she and her husband lost their jobs and their home was bombed.

For Hamer, political activism became a way of life. She organized citizenship schools and helped others to register. She endured brutal beatings in jail. And she helped found the Freedom Democratic party, which challenged Mississippi's all-white delegation to the 1964 Democratic National Convention.

Hamer did not succeed in the delegate challenge of 1964. But between 1968 and 1974, the Democratic party wrote new rules governing the choosing of delegates and the conduct of presidential primaries. Those rules gave greater representation to women's rights activists, social justice seekers, and civil rights workers. Many believe that Hamer's efforts helped to trigger those changes.

During the mid-1960s, the civil rights movement ceased being nonviolent. The Vietnamese War was raging. Its scenes of death and destruction were a central feature of nightly news telecasts. A church in Birmingham, Alabama, was bombed, and four little girls lost their lives. Working to register black voters in the summer of 1964, Andrew Goodman and Michael Schwerner, two whites from the North, and James Chaney, a black southerner, were murdered.

In February 1965, Malcolm X was gunned down. A month later, as thousands of civil rights activists led by Martin Luther King, Jr., walked from Selma to Montgomery, Alabama, a white civil rights worker from Detroit named Viola Liuzzo was shot and killed by four members of the Ku Klux Klan, a secret society organized in the South after the Civil War to support white supremacy, often using terrorist methods.

The civil rights movement transformed many parts of the South. It helped put an end to public segregation and the humiliation it caused. It integrated school systems and boosted the number and involvement of black voters.

The civil rights movement and the student antiwar demonstrations also helped to inspire women to launch a new struggle for equal rights. "Freedom now!" black activists had proclaimed. The women's movement of the early 1970s would have the same sense of urgency.

The Southern Rural Women Network joins in a protest march in Alabama.

Esther Peterson, named by President Kennedy to head the Commission on the Status of Women.

The New Feminism

There have been two major women's movements in the United States, two waves of feminist activity that have produced deep social change. The first, concerned with suffrage and the abolition of slavery, ended with the passage of the Nineteenth Amendment in 1920.

The second, which began in the 1960s and continues through the present day, has had far greater impact. It has changed people's views about marriage, family life, and the workplace, and the way men and women view their lives. No aspect of American life has been left untouched.

The seeds for change were sown in the

Betty Friedan, who wrote The Feminine Mystique *in 1962.*

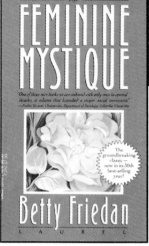

The Feminine Mystique *helped spark thousands of American women to change their lives.*

1960s. After John F. Kennedy became president in 1961, one of his first acts was to form the Commission on the Status of Women. As the commission's chairperson, Kennedy named Eleanor Roosevelt, then in her seventies. After her husband's death in 1945, Mrs. Roosevelt had continued to work for human rights. As the U.S. Delegate to the United Nations in 1946, and chairperson of the U.N. Commission on Human Rights, Mrs. Roosevelt had played a major role in the drafting of the Universal Declaration of Human Rights, adopted by the U.N. in 1948. President Kennedy named Esther Petersen as the director of the Commission on the Status of Women.

The commission's final report, issued in 1963, spelled out the many inequalities women had to deal with. These included discrimination in employment and unequal pay, plus a lack of social services, such as child care.

One direct result of the commission's findings was the Equal Pay Act, passed by Congress in 1963. The legislation made it illegal for an employer to have different rates of pay for women and men who did the same work. Another step forward was a presidential order issued by Kennedy that required the Civil Service to hire "solely on the basis of ability to meet the requirements of the position, and without regard to sex."

The same year the Commission on the Status of Women issued its report, a book was published that was to have a startling effect on American women. Titled *The Feminine Mystique*, its author was Betty Friedan. In her book, Friedan urged women to reject society's idea that limited them to roles as wives and mothers. She called upon women to return to colleges and professional schools to seek and develop careers of their own.

The Feminine Mystique had its faults. The book was directed to white, well-educated, middle-class women. It had little meaning for working-class women or minority women. Their problems were much more serious than the ones cited by Friedan. And Friedan's book ignored the fact that homemaking and motherhood were deeply satisfying to many American women.

Despite its shortcomings, *The Feminine Mystique* awakened millions of American women. They were relieved to be told that they were not alone in their feelings of boredom and isolation. They were ready to make a change in their lives.

At the time, organized feminism was at a standstill. Friedan's book helped to inject new life into the movement.

Just as women were beginning to develop a greater concern for economic and social equality, they were suddenly handed a powerful weapon that could be used as protection against discrimination.

On June 29, 1964, the U.S. Senate passed an all-embracing Civil Rights Bill. It outlawed discrimination in public accommodations, union membership, and jobs. The bill helped guarantee African-Americans the right to vote. Previously passed by the House of Representatives, the bill was signed into law by President Lyndon B. Johnson on July 2, 1964.

"The passage of the Civil Rights Bill may well be the single most important act of Congress in several decades," said James L. Farmer, national director of CORE, the Congress of Racial Equality. "It gives hope to Negroes that the American people and government mean to redeem the promise of the Declaration of Independence and the Emancipation Proclamation."

At the urging of Alice Paul and other activists, Title VII of the Civil Rights Act, which outlawed discrimination on the basis of "race, color, religion, or national origin," was amended to include the word "sex." Women were thus handed a powerful tool with which to fight discrimination.

It didn't take women long to discover that they needed an organization to enforce the provisions of Title VII. For example, women protested newspaper "Help Wanted" ads, which, at the time,

Members of the National Organization for Women work on posters in NOW's New York offices, in preparation for Women's March for Equality, held on August 26, 1971.

classified some jobs strictly for "male" workers, while others were only for those who were "female." Feminists declared such ads to be as discriminatory as those that distinguished between black and white workers. Yet the Equal Employment Opportunity Commission (EEOC), the government agency set up to deal with such complaints, saw nothing wrong with the ads.

The realization on the part of women that they needed an organization that would demand enforcement of the laws banning discrimination on the basis of sex led to the formation of NOW — the National Organization for Women. "It took only a few of us to get together to ignite the spark," Betty Friedan later wrote, "and it spread like a nuclear chain reaction."

NOW was born in 1966. In some ways, the organization and its goals could be compared to those set in Seneca Falls, New York, more than a century before. In both cases, equal participation and individual rights for women were called for.

In its statement of purpose, NOW declared it was not only time for women to share in the male world of politics, business, and the professions, but it was also time for men to start sharing in the women's sphere. Said NOW: "We believe that a true partnership between the sexes demands a different concept of marriage, an equitable sharing of the responsibilities of home and children and of the economic burdens of support." With a membership of over 250,000, NOW is today the largest feminist organization in the United States.

The Women's Equity Action League

Women's March for Equality, held in New York during the summer of 1971, drew nearly 5,000 participants.

Members of the National Women's Political Caucus announced in 1972 that one of their goals was to have women make up half the delegates to the Democratic and Republican presidential nominating conventions held that year. From left are: Gloria Steinem, a member of the Democratic National Policy Council at the time; Rep. Shirley Chisholm of New York; Betty Friedan; and, standing, Rep. Bella Abzug of New York.

(WEAL), founded in 1968, is another women's rights organization active today. A watchdog agency, the League monitors educational institutions and businesses to detect discriminatory practices in pay and promotion. When it finds unfair performance, WEAL acts. In 1970, WEAL filed complaints of sex discrimination against some 300 colleges and universities. The schools were threatened with the loss of federal funds they had been receiving unless they began to hire and promote more women.

Another organization, Federally Employed Women (FEW), founded in 1968, seeks to end job discrimination in government service. The National Women's Political Caucus (NWPC), established in 1971, is meant to strengthen women's political influence on local,

state, and national levels. By the early 1990s, the NWPC had more than 75,000 members.

Today, these and some fifty other women's organizations are active on a national level. Achieving legislative, educational, and economic equality for women is their goal.

The first feminist movement, in which women fought for suffrage and the abolition of slavery, lasted more than a century. By comparison, the present movement has had a short life. Gloria Steinem, a journalist who was in the forefront of the feminist movement during the late 1960s, noted in 1993, "We're about twenty-five years into this wave, with about seventy-five years to go.

"Then there'll probably be another wave."

Women described as "women's liberationists" march into Harvard Square in Cambridge, Massachusetts, in 1971. They had just evacuated a Harvard University building they had occupied for 10 days.

Women's Liberation

Gehan Kelley, co-owner of the Sisterhood Bookstore in the Woman's Building in Los Angeles, displays a "Wonder Woman" T-shirt in 1972, described as one of the biggest selling items in the store.

The feminist movement of the 1960s advanced by leaps and bounds along several different fronts. One was traditional, and leaned heavily on NOW and the work of other such organizations. Called mainstream feminism, it was concerned with the struggle by women to achieve economic, political, legal, and social rights equal to men.

A second thrust involved poor women of all races whose chief concerns were such issues as child-care centers and welfare rights.

A third grouping was made up of younger, angrier, and more defiant women. It came to be called the women's liberation movement.

Women's liberation was started by women students who had been active in the anti-war and civil rights movements and who opposed the "power structure" of existing organizations (rather like the way in which Elizabeth Cady Stanton

During the late 1960s, the title Ms. before a woman's name, equivalent to Mr. before a man's name, began to be heard. Heated debate surrounded its use. In 1972, when the first issue of <u>Ms.</u> magazine appeared, it helped widen acceptance of the term. Gloria Steinem (left) was the magazine's founder; Pat Carbine, its editor.

and Lucretia Mott became dissatisfied with the leadership of the anti-slavery movement). Men were in charge of these organizations; women were expected to make coffee, type, and run errands.

At a peace demonstration in Washington, DC, early in 1968, women's liberation turned a corner. Leaders of the movement sought to convince other women that until they dealt with their own status they would be unable to solve any other problems of society. The slogan "Sisterhood of Power" was heard for the first time.

In September that year, during the Miss America pageant in Atlantic City, the women's liberation movement exploded into the national consciousness. There were loud and angry demonstrations against sexism (discrimination of a person based on sex) and the display of women as sex objects. Women dumped girdles, bras, cosmetics, and high-heeled shoes in a "freedom trash can." One result was daily newspaper and television coverage. Suddenly, women and men everywhere were aware of the women's movement.

During these formative years, Gloria Steinem, a journalist based in New York City, emerged as one of the leading figures of the movement. While Steinem became best known as one of the founding editors of *Ms.* magazine, the most widely read of all feminist publications, she was also, in 1971, co-founder of the Women's Action Alliance. The WAA develops educational programs and services to assist women and their organizations in achieving full equality. Steinem is also well known for articles and books she has written on such topics as politics, women and work, and the Equal Rights Amendment.

By the early 1970s, everyone was talking about "women's lib." And no wonder; the tactics used by radical feminists grabbed headlines. They conducted speak-outs, disrupted congressional hearings, and announced the availability of self-defense karate classes for women.

On March 18, 1970, 200 women occupied the offices of the *Ladies Home Journal*. They demanded the magazine replace its male editor with a female, hire more minorities, and provide day care for its employees.

The women's liberation movement had no president or national headquarters, no constitution or membership list. It consisted of thousands of small groups of women that met weekly to take part in an educational process known as consciousness-raising. Discussions might concern such topics as housework or office work, husbands and marriages, or childhood experiences and mother-daughter relationships. Women spoke about their own experiences.

Through consciousness-raising, group members were able to gain an awareness of discrimination in society. Consciousness-raising also sought to make one's personal life political, and thereby achieve the ultimate goal,

Gradually women began to break into jobs traditionally held by men, like this female firefighter.

A female construction worker at work in the shadow of the Capitol.

which was to make change.

As a result of the feminist movement, women began to score one success after another. Early in 1970, *The New York Times* declared in a front-page article: "The walls of economic and psychological discrimination against women in the American job market are beginning to crack under the pressures of the Federal government, the women's liberation movement, and the efforts of thousands of individual women themselves."

During the 1970s, two women were elected governors. A black Congresswoman, Barbara Jordan, was the keynote speaker at the 1976 Democratic Convention.

Women themselves changed, too. They became more confident. Women began telephoning men to ask for dates. Women started paying their own way to the movies and half the dinner check. Women who had no wish to marry felt free not to do so.

As the women's movement kept growing, the differences that divided the older branch of the movement, as represented by NOW and other national organizations, and the women's liberationists kept fading away. Women from both groups realized that their ultimate goals weren't so different. Different factors still exist today, but their attitudes, values, and tactics are more similar.

Ella Grasso of Connecticut, the first woman elected governor in the United States. Here she gives a victory sign after voting in the town of Windsor Locks in 1974.

Beginning in the 1970s and into the 1990s, Barbara Walters reigned as one of TV's foremost journalists.

First Women

Once the modern feminist movement gained a foothold, women began to record one breakthrough achievement after another. Their accomplishments occurred in every field, from sports to politics, from science to show business. It would take a book at least the size of this one to tell the stories of all of the pioneering women of the last 20 to 30 years. Some of the most notable include:

Ella Grasso: A member of the U.S. Congress from Connecticut from 1971 to 1975, Ella Grasso made history in 1975 when she became the first woman elected governor in the United States. When Connecticut voters overwhelmingly returned her to office in 1978, she became the first woman ever re-elected governor.

Barbara Walters: A writer on NBC's *Today* show, and later a television co-

Sandra Day O'Connor, the first woman justice of the Supreme Court. Here she poses with Chief Justice Warren Burger before swearing in ceremonies in 1981.

host, Walters made headlines in 1976 by teaming with Harry Reasoner as a newscaster on the *ABC Evening News*. She thus became the first woman to co-anchor a daily evening news program. For signing, Walters received the record-breaking salary of $1 million a year. In 1992, Walters became the first TV personality to be honored by the American Museum of the Moving Image for her outstanding contributions to television.

Sandra Day O'Connor: Described by President Ronald Reagan as a person with "unique qualities of temperament, fairness, and intellectual capacity,"

O'Connor, on July 7, 1981, was introduced by the president as his first nominee to the Supreme Court. When the U.S. Senate confirmed her appointment on September 21 that year, O'Connor became the first woman justice of the Supreme Court.

Sally Ride: One of the first women selected as an astronaut, Ride became the first American woman to travel in space on June 18, 1983, when the space shuttle *Challenger* was launched from the Kennedy Space Center at Cape Canaveral, Florida. Ride also flew as a mission specialist on STS 41-G, launched from the Cape on October

On June 18, 1983, Sally Ride became the first American woman to travel in space.

In the Olympic Games in 1984, when the first marathon for women was held, the gold medal went to Joan Benoit of Freeport, Maine.

5, 1984. With the completion of that mission, Ride had logged slightly more than 14 days in space.

Joan Benoit: As recently as 1980, there was no race longer than a mile for women in the Olympic Games. In 1984, when a women's marathon was offered for the first time, Benoit, from Freeport, Maine, won the 26-mile, 385-yard event, running the distance in 2 hours, 24 minutes, 52 seconds.

Dr. Mae Jemison: A physician from Houston, Texas, Jemison was chosen as the first black woman astronaut in 1987. "Not only is she highly qualified technically," said Dr. Joseph D. Atkin-son, Jr., chief of NASA's Equal Opportunity Programs Office, "but she is also extremely sensitive to the social needs of the community. I would call Dr. Jemison a real national asset."

Antonia Novella: As a child growing up in Puerto Rico, Novella dreamed of becoming "a pediatrician — a doctor for little kids in my hometown." In 1990, with a master's degree in public health from Johns Hopkins University in Baltimore, Novella became "a doctor for all Americans" when she was sworn in at the White House as the nation's surgeon general. She was the first woman ever to be appointed to the post.

In 1987, Dr. Mae Jemison, a physician from Houston, became the first black female astronaut.

Antonia Novella, the first woman to be named surgeon general of the United States. President George Bush appointed Novella to the post in 1990.

A pair of women on stilts were among the thousands of women who marched in Washington, DC, in 1978 to show their support for the Equal Rights Amendment.

In May, 1978, Barbara Jordan tells a House Judiciary Committee that she favors extension of the ratification period for the proposed Equal Rights Amendment.

The Equal Rights Amendment

The modern feminist movement has achieved many breakthroughs for women. A good number of them have been legislative in nature. During the 1970s, Congress passed an unprecedented number of laws intended to improve the status of women.

Title IX of the Higher Education Act of 1972, for example, bans discrimination on the basis of sex on the part of schools and colleges receiving federal funds. The law applies not only to school and college admissions policies, but also to educational, recreational, and athletic programs.

The Equal Opportunity Act, which went into effect in 1975, prevents stores, banks, and other such institutions from discriminating on the basis of sex or marital status when issuing credit cards or making loans.

But not every effort to change existing

laws or write new ones has been successful. The Equal Rights Amendment is a case in point.

Called the ERA for short, the amendment was drafted by Alice Paul, one of the first activists for equal rights for women. Sometimes called the mother of the Equal Rights Amendment, Paul was active much earlier in organizing protests calling for the government to grant voting rights to women. In 1917, she was jailed for picketing the White House.

After the passage of the suffrage amendment in 1920, Paul devoted her energies toward achieving legal equality for women. She drafted the Equal Rights Amendment and submitted it to Congress in 1923. The wording was revised slightly in 1944. The complete text reads:

Section I: Equality of rights under the law shall not be denied or abridged by the United States or by any State on account of sex.

Section II: The Congress shall have the power to enforce, by appropriate legislation, the provisions of this article.

Section III: This amendment shall take effect two years after the date of ratification.

Critics of the amendment said that the Constitution already guaranteed equal rights to women. They also played on people's fears, saying that passage of the amendment would mean that women would be drafted into the armed services in the event of war. They said it would mean the end of separate toilets in restaurants, theaters, and other public

Some of the estimated 50,000 to 100,000 marchers that took part in the ERA demonstration in Washington, DC, in 1978. They urged Congress to extend the time for ratification of the amendment.

Supporters of the Equal Rights Amendment parade at the NOW convention in Washington, DC, in 1981.

places. They said the ERA would end the right of a wife to be supported by her husband.

Those who supported the ERA pointed out that existing laws have failed to give women basic employment and educational opportunities equal to those available to men. They also said that the amendment would have no affect upon the relationship of a wife and husband within their marriage.

After years of debate, the Equal Rights Amendment was passed by Congress in 1972, then sent to the states for ratification. Hawaii was the first state to ratify the amendment; Nebraska was second. By the end of 1973, thirty states had passed the amendment. Passage was required in eight more states for the amendment to become a part of the Constitution.

Congress required that the ERA, like most amendments, be ratified within seven years. That meant that the supporters of the ERA had until March 22, 1979, to obtain ratification in the 38 states. When they failed to meet that deadline, Congress voted to extend it until June 30, 1982. By the 1982 deadline, only 35 of the 38 states had ratified the amendment, and the chance for an equal rights amendment had been lost.

During the 1980s and into the 1990s, the National Women's party continued to work to get the Equal Rights Amendment reintroduced in Congress, but without a ratification deadline. Women are still not treated equally in our society, despite the guarantees of the Constitution, say supporters of the ERA. Enactment and ratification of the ERA are essential to achieve such equality.

Geraldine Ferraro campaigns in 1985. A Democrat, Ferraro was the first woman to be named a candidate for vice president by a major political party.

Women in Office

In winning reelection to the U.S. Senate in 1992, Maryland's Barbara Mikulski got 76 percent of the female vote.

In 1992, a presidential election year that saw Bill Clinton defeat George Bush, women made history at the ballot box. For the first time, they voted in significant numbers in support of female candidates and women's issues. The result was that historic numbers of women were propelled into political office. In Maryland, for example, Senator Barbara Mikulski won reelection with 76 percent of the female vote (and 66 percent of the male vote).

Always before, women and men had voted pretty much alike. One person who knows this to be true is Geraldine Ferraro, who, in 1984, was selected by Democrat Walter F. Mondale to be his vice-presidential running mate, becoming the first woman to be named by a major political party as a candidate for vice president. Ferraro once recalled that during the campaign she received contributions for her campaign fund from women and little notes saying, "I don't want my husband to know, but I'm supporting you." Then on Election Day, says Ferraro, they "voted the same as the men." The Mondale–Ferraro ticket was soundly beaten by Republicans Ronald Reagan and George Bush.

In 1992, with women voting the gender line, the number of women in the U.S. Senate jumped by 200 percent, or four seats. In the House of Representatives, the number of women increased by 68 percent, or 19 seats. However, in actual numbers, women in Congress are still a very distinct minority. When the One-hundred-third Congress convened in January 1993, women held only 6 of the 100 seats in the Senate and 48 of the 435 seats in the House.

Clinton also appointed three women cabinet members — Janet Reno, Donna Shalala, and Hazel R. O'Leary — as well as Surgeon General Joycelyn Elders and Supreme Court Justice Ruth Ginsburg.

But the woman with the greatest im-

In 1993, women held six of the 100 seats in the U.S. Senate. One belonged to Carol Moseley Braun of Illinois.

President Clinton made no secret of the fact that he frequently turned to his wife, Hillary, for advice and counsel.

Janet Reno is sworn in as Attorney General in 1993, as President Clinton looks on.

pact on the Clinton administration is the president's wife, Hillary Rodham Clinton, to whom he often turns for advice and counsel. Twice named one of the 100 top lawyers in the United States, Hillary Clinton is looked upon as an expert on family, health, and educational issues. Upon taking office, the president announced that Hillary Clinton would oversee the administration's plan to reform the nation's healthcare system, considered one of Clinton's biggest challenges.

The year 1992 was designated The Year of the Woman. As it was drawing to a close, women's gains for the year, or lack of them, were evaluated. On the political front, many feminists saw only a slight advance. "Tripling our representation in the Senate," said one, "is no triumph when the female faces go from two to six."

And Gloria Steinem added: "It will not be the year of the woman until we have half of the House and half of the Senate and a president once in a while."

President Bill Clinton signs the Family and Medical Leave Act early in February 1993. This legislation gave many workers the right to take unpaid leaves of up to 12 weeks for family emergencies, including the birth of a child or to care for a child, spouse, or parent with a serious health condition. Looking on is Vicki Yandle of Marietta, Georgia. Mrs. Yandle lost her job because she took time off when her daughter was sick.

Women and the Future

Thanks to the women's movement and the social revolution it brought forth, a vast majority of Americans now supports the idea of equality for women. But women don't have equality yet.

There is much to be accomplished. The three branches of government (legislative, judicial, and executive) are still heavily male, middle-aged, white, and wealthy.

While other nations have had female leaders, such as Indira Gandhi (India),

Golda Meir (Israel), Corazon Aquino (The Philippines), Margaret Thatcher (Great Britain), and Benazir Bhutto (Pakistan), it is not likely a woman will be elected president of the United States for many years to come.

The goals set forth by women's organizations have shifted somewhat in recent years. Now, social welfare legislation is being sought. There is a push for new laws to provide for early childhood development and before- and after-school quality care. Social welfare bills providing for parental leave from work for pregnancy and childbirth, which were championed by women's organizations during the 1980s and early 1990s, were signed into law by President Bill Clinton early in 1993.

Women's organizations have also become more concerned about the rights of older women. NOW, for example, is dedicated to providing economic protection for older women, who, says a NOW

Women dressed in traditional suffragist clothing, participating in NOW's "March for Equality" in 1987, walk past Independence Hall in Philadelphia.

*"Now let's get to work" was the message to women
at the inauguration of President Clinton in 1993.*

spokesperson, ". . . all too often are condemned to a life of poverty."

The Social Security system, says NOW, is guilty of sex discrimination by providing payments to women that amount to less than 60 percent of what men average. NOW is working to change Social Security unfairness and also discriminatory practices in health insurance plans and pension and retirement programs.

The nation's labor force reflects the most dramatic changes wrought by the women's movement. In 1940, 28 percent of women were employed; by 1990, the number had jumped to almost 60 percent.

But there is still a yawning gap in salaries between men and women. As of the early 1990s, according to the Bureau of Labor Statistics, the average woman earned 71 cents for every dollar a man earned.

And despite the fact that women have moved into countless jobs that were once considered for males only, nearly half of all women workers are still employed in these ten occupations: secretary, salesclerk, domestic, elementary schoolteacher, bookkeeper, waitress, stitcher and sewer, cashier, and typist.

Feminists are well aware of this situation. In 1993, partly to give girls a chance to gain an appreciation of the

Women have taken on countless jobs once filled by men almost exclusively. These six female pilots got their First Officer wings from Texas International Airlines in 1978.

many different career opportunities available to them, the Ms. Foundation designated April 28 as Take Our Daughters to Work Day. Girls from 9 to 15 years old were taken along to work by a parent or friend. Hundreds of thousands of girls participated in what will become an annual event.

When it comes to jobs and income, households headed by single mothers occupy the bottom rungs of the ladder. In 1991, a startling 46 percent of all families headed by single mothers lived below the poverty line.

While men take a more active role in parenting today, child care and household labor are still looked upon as women's work. "We are trying to change our roles but we are all stuck in tradition," says Joyce Poster, a New York psychotherapist. "Life is very different from what it has ever been, but people still have the same expectations of each other. I say women have double-trouble; they have careers but are expected to come home and cook and clean."

Few people oppose the concept of equality for women. But the basic changes needed to make that idea a reality still attract opposition. There are plenty of issues that remain to be addressed, plenty of battles still to be fought.

Important Dates in Women's Struggle for Equal Rights

....

1655
Lady Deborah Moody of Long Island, New York, is allowed to vote in a town meeting, a rare instance of woman suffrage in the colonies.

1792
British author Mary Wollstonecraft calls for women's equality with men in her book *A Vindication of the Rights of Women.*

1839
February 16 — Kentucky state legislature grants suffrage to widows with children of school age.

1840
World Anti-Slavery Convention held in London. American women delegates are prohibited from attending convention sessions, triggering women's rights movement in the United States.

1848
July 19 and 20 — First Women's Rights Convention held at Seneca Falls, New York, by Lucretia Mott and Elizabeth Cady Stanton.

1849
Elizabeth Blackwell receives medical degree from Geneva College, New York, to become the first American woman physician.

1850
October 23 and 24 — First National Women's Rights Convention held in Worcester, Massachusetts.

1851
Amelia Bloomer, in her magazine, *The Lily*, launches campaign for women's dress reform.

1853
September 15 — Antoinette L. Brown, a Congregationalist, from South Butler, New York, becomes the first U.S. woman to be ordained a minister.

1860
March 19 — Elizabeth Cady Stanton addresses joint session of New York State Legislature on the subject of women's suffrage.

1865
For her service to the Union army as a medical officer during the Civil War, Dr. Mary Walker is awarded the Medal of Honor, the only woman ever to receive the award.

1866
American Equal Rights Association founded to further the interests of blacks and women.

1869
March 15 — Women's suffrage amendment to the Constitution proposed in joint resolution to Congress.
May 15 — National Woman Suffrage Association formed in New York City, with Elizabeth Cady Stanton as president.
November 24 — American Woman Suffrage Association founded in Cleveland, with Henry Ward Beecher as president.
December 10 — Wyoming Territory grants suffrage to women.

1870
February 12 — Territory of Utah grants suffrage to women.

1873
Eliza Daniel Stewart founds the Woman's Temperance League, a forerunner of the Woman's Christian Temperance Union.

1874
Woman's Christian Temperance Union founded in Cleveland, Ohio.

1875
May 8 — Massachusetts enacts the first effective 10-hour workday law for women.

1879

February 15 — Belva Lockwood becomes the first woman lawyer admitted to practice before the U.S. Supreme Court.

1889

Territory of Wyoming admitted to the Union; thus Wyoming becomes the first state with voting rights for women.

1890

February 18 — National and American Woman Suffrage Association formed out of merger of two organizations, American Woman Suffrage Association and National Woman Suffrage Association.

1894

November 7 — Colorado adopts women's suffrage by popular vote.

1896

November 3 — Idaho grants women's suffrage by constitutional amendment.

1908

January 21 — Sullivan Ordinance passed in New York City, making smoking by women in public places illegal.
February 24 — In *Muller* v. *State of Oregon*, the U.S. Supreme Court upholds Oregon's 10-hour-day law for women in industry.
March 8 — International Women's Day celebrated for the first time.

1910

State of Washington adopts women's suffrage by constitutional amendment.

1911

October 10 — California adopts women's suffrage by constitutional amendment.

1912

January 12 — Proposed women's suffrage amendment defeated in U.S. House of Representatives.
Massachusetts adopts minimum wage law for women and children, nation's first such legislation.
States of Arizona, Kansas, and Oregon grant suffrage to women.

1913

State of Illinois grants voting rights to women in presidential elections. Territory of Alaska grants voting rights to women. National Woman's Party founded by Alice Paul out of merger of Congressional Union for Woman Suffrage and Woman's Party.

1914

March 3 — Suffragists march in Washington, DC.
States of Montana and Nevada grant voting rights to women.

1916

Jeannette Rankin, a Republican from Montana, is elected to the House of Representatives to become the first female member of Congress.

1917

October 27 — Twenty-thousand women march in suffrage parade in New York City.
Suffrage granted to women by the states of North Dakota, Ohio, Indiana, Rhode Island, Nebraska, Michigan, and New York. State of Arkansas granted women the right to vote in primary elections.

1918

October 1 — Resolution providing for Women's Suffrage Amendment rejected by U.S. Senate for third time. Resolution was passed by the House of Representatives on January 10.

1919

June 5 — The Nineteenth Amendment to the Constitution granting suffrage to women adopted by joint resolution of Congress and sent to the states for ratification.
League of Women Voters, organization that evolved out of National American Woman Suffrage Association, founded in Washington, DC.

1920

August 18 — Tennessee becomes the thirty-sixth and final state to ratify the Nineteenth Amendment.
August 26 — The Nineteenth Amendment, granting suffrage to women, proclaimed to be in effect.

1923
Equal Rights Amendment, as drafted by Alice Paul, introduced in Congress for the first time.

1925
April 18 — The first women's worlds' fair, known officially as "The World Exposition of Women's Progress," opens in Chicago.

1931
Jane Addams becomes the first woman to win the Nobel Peace Prize. Founder of the Women's International League for Peace and Freedom in 1915, Addams received the award for her lifetime of dedication to the cause of peace and justice.

1932
November 8 — Democrat Hattie Wyatt Caraway of Arkansas becomes the first woman to be elected to the U.S. Senate.

1933
Frances C. Perkins, named Secretary of Labor by Franklin D. Roosevelt, becomes the first woman cabinet member.

1942
May 14 — Women's Army Auxiliary Corps (WAAC) established by Act of Congress.
July 30 — Women authorized to serve in U.S. Navy by Act of Congress. They are designated WAVES — Women Appointed for Volunteer Emergency Service.
November 23 — Women's division of U.S. Coast Guard — SPARS — created by Act of Congress.

1948
Women's Army Corps established as part of Regular Army.

1951
Marguerite (Maggie) Higgins of the *New York Herald Tribune*, becomes the first woman to win the Pulitzer Prize for International Reporting.

1953
September 15 — H. E. Ms.

Vijayalakshmi Pandit of India becomes the first woman elected president of the United Nations General Assembly.

1961
December 14 — President John F. Kennedy establishes the President's Commission on the Status of Women.

1963
June 10 — Congress enacts legislation guaranteeing women equal pay for equal work.
Betty Friedan's book, *The Feminine Mystique*, is published.

1964
July 2 — Civil Rights Act signed into law by President Lyndon B. Johnson.

1966
The National Organization for Women, the largest organization dedicated to insuring equal rights for women, founded in Washington, DC, with Betty Friedan as its first president.

1968
Organization of Federally Employed Women founded in Washington, DC.

1969
Center for Women's Studies and Services founded in San Diego, California.

1971
National Women's Political Caucus founded in Washington, DC.
National Black Women's Political Leadership Caucus founded in Washington, DC.

1972
Title IX of the Higher Education Act of 1972 goes into effect, banning discrimination on the basis of sex in schools and colleges receiving federal funds.
Ms. Foundation for Women, with goals of eliminating sex discrimination and improving the status of women and girls, founded in New York City.
November 15 — Jeanne Martin Cisse of Guinea becomes the first woman elected to preside over the United Nations Security Council.

1973
Nine to Five, National Association of Working Women, founded in Cleveland, Ohio.

1975
October 29 — Nationwide strike by women called by the National Organization for Women. Women march and stage protests in New York, Los Angeles, Washington, Philadelphia, Detroit, and other cities to demonstrate their refusal to support an "oppressive, sexist system."
The Equal Opportunity Act goes into effect, preventing stores, banks, and other such institutions from discriminating on the basis of sex or marital status when issuing credit cards or making loans.

1978
International Women's Day — March 8 — included in list of holidays officially recognized by the United Nations.

1981
Sandra Day O'Connor named first woman justice of the U.S. Supreme Court. National Coalition of 100 Black Women formed in New York City.

1984
Geraldine Ferraro, a Democrat, becomes the first woman nominated by a major political party as a candidate for vice president of the United States.

1993
February 5 — President Bill Clinton signs the Family Leave Bill.
April 28 — *Ms.* Foundation for Women schedules first annual Take Our Daughters to Work Day.

92

For Further Reading

Young Readers

Cullen-Dupont, Kathryn. *Elizabeth Cady Stanton & Women's Liberty*. New York: Facts on File, 1992.

Hammer, Trudy J. *Taking a Stand Against Sexism & Sex Discrimination*. New York: Franklin Watts, 1990.

Hoff, Mark. *Gloria Steinem: The Women's Movement*. Brookfield, Connecticut: Millbrook Press, 1991.

Meltzer, Milton. *Betty Friedan: A Voice for Women's Rights*. New York: Viking Books, 1985.

Rapport, Doreen. *American Women, Their Lives in Their Words*. New York: Thomas Y. Crowell, 1990.

Read, Phyllis J., and Bernard L. Witlieb. *The Book of Women's Firsts*. New York: Random House, 1992.

Smith, Betsy C. *Women Win the Vote*. Englewood Cliffs, New Jersey: Silver Burdett Press, 1989.

Tuttle, Lisa. *Encyclopedia of Feminism*. New York: Facts on File, 1986.

Young-Adult Readers

Burnett, Constance B. *Five for Freedom: Lucretia Mott, Elizabeth Cady Stanton, Lucy Stone, Susan B. Anthony, Carrie Chapman Catt*. Westport, Connecticut: Greenwood Press, 1968.

Cleverdon, Catherine L. *The Woman Suffrage Movement in Canada: The Start of Liberation*. Toronto: University of Toronto Press, 1974.

Evans, Sara M. *Born for Liberty: A History of Women in America*. New York: The Free Press, 1989.

Flexner, Eleanor. *Century of Struggle: The Women's Rights Movement in the United States*. New York: Atheneum, 1973.

Foner, Philip S. *Frederick Douglass on Women's Rights*. Westport, Connecticut: Greenwood Press, 1976.

Friedan, Betty. *The Feminine Mystique*. New York: Norton & Co., 1983.

Gluck, Sherna, ed. *From Parlor to Prison: Five American Suffragists Talk About Their Lives*. New York: Hippocrene Books, 1976.

Hymovitz, Carol, and Michaele Weissman. *A History of Women in America*. New York: Bantam Books, 1978.

Ramelson, Marian. *Petticoat Rebellion: A Century of Struggle for Women's Rights*. Woodstock, New York: Beekman Publications, 1976.

Rubenstein, David. *Before the Suffragettes: Women's Emancipation in the 1890s*. New York: St. Martin's Press, 1986.

Wollstonecraft, Mary. *Vindication of the Rights of Woman*. New York: Alfred A. Knopf, 1992.

Index